Runaway

The Daring Escape
of Ona Judge

Written by **Ray Anthony Shepard**

Illustrated by **Keith Mallett**

Farrar Straus Giroux
New York

Farrar Straus Giroux Books for Young Readers
An imprint of Macmillan Publishing Group, LLC
120 Broadway, New York, NY 10271

Text copyright © 2021 by Ray Anthony Shepard
Illustrations copyright © 2021 by Keith Mallett
All rights reserved
Color separations by Bright Arts (H.K.) Ltd.
Printed in China by RR Donnelley Asia Printing Solutions Ltd., Dongguan City, Guangdong Province
Designed by Aram Kim
First edition, 2021
3 5 7 9 10 8 6 4 2

Library of Congress Cataloging-in-Publication Data

Names: Shepard, Ray Anthony, author. | Mallett, Keith, illustrator.
Title: Runaway : the daring escape of Ona Judge / Ray Anthony Shepard ;
[illustrated by] Keith Mallett.
Other titles: Daring escape of Ona Judge
Description: New York, New York : Farrar Straus Giroux Books for Young
Readers, [2021] | Audience: Ages 4–8 | Audience: Grades 2–3 | Summary:
An elegant, unforgiving poem narrating Ona Judge's self-emancipation
from George Washington's household— Provided by publisher.
Identifiers: LCCN 2020018822 | ISBN 9780374307042 (hardcover)
Subjects: LCSH: Judge, Ona—Juvenile literature. | Fugitive slaves—United
States—Biography—Juvenile literature. | Slaves—United
States—Biography—Juvenile literature. | African American
women—Biography—Juvenile literature. | African
Americans—Biography—Juvenile literature. | Racially mixed
women—United States—Biography—Juvenile literature. | Washington,
Martha, 1731-1802—Relations with slaves—Juvenile literature. |
Washington, George, 1732-1799—Relations with slaves—Juvenile
literature.
Classification: LCC E450.S545 2021 | DDC 973.4/1092 [B]—dc23
LC record available at https://lccn.loc.gov/2020018822

Our books may be purchased in bulk for promotional, educational, or business use. Please contact your local bookseller or the Macmillan
Corporate and Premium Sales Department at (800) 221-7945 ext. 5442 or by email at MacmillanSpecialMarkets@macmillan.com.

Elizabeth, you are the great, great, great granddaughter of many daring ancestors who dreamed of the life you now live. May you always be blessed with the courage of Ona.

Love, Pop Pop —R.A.S.

To Dianne, Chris, and Nia!
—K.M.

Ona Judge, Ona Judge

Why you run away

Ona Judge?

You had fine dresses

Fancy bonnets for your bushy black hair

Soft shoes on your tender brown feet

Why you run Ona Judge?

You rode in a first-class carriage
With the lady who called you her own

On Cherry Street

She took you to the best houses

When she visited other important ladies

Why you run Ona Judge?

You were the lady's favorite

She carried you off from Mount Vernon when you were sixteen

Didn't ask if you wanted to go

Didn't ask you if you would miss your mama

She hauled you to New York
To brush her hair

She towed you
to Philadelphia
To sew her elegant gowns
Why you run Ona Judge?

You ate the food
Hercules cooked for the lady's husband,
George Washington

You had your own room in the President's House
With a fireplace and servants to bring you wood
Why you run Ona Judge?

You were the color of saltwater caramel
With freckles of cinnamon flakes
Your hair the scent of dogwood
Your eyes, dark like British coal

On Chestnut Street men tipped their hats
To you and Eliza, the president's granddaughter,
They thought you were her friend
　　Why you run Ona Judge?

You saw history at the dining room table

When you peeked through the kitchen door

Thomas Jefferson, John Adams, Alexander Hamilton

Warriors and diplomats
Who made America free
Did you think they meant you?

You didn't work in the buckwheat fields

Your hands stayed soft
Your clothes kept clean
Why you run Ona Judge?

The lady read you stories from the Bible
Told you her problems
She didn't teach you to read
Or show you how to write

Wanted you the way you were

Her pet

Her darling slave

    Why you run Ona Judge?

Didn't you know you belonged to the lady?

Like her favorite chair, or a pair of silk stockings

She was getting old

Wanted to keep you in the family

Gave you to her granddaughter Eliza . . .

Eliza, the girl you played with when you were ten

And she was seven

Now a mean and sassy woman

Would keep you in fine dresses

Fancy bonnets and soft shoes
Let you rock her babies to sleep
Why you run Ona Judge?

But you walked out the door

Ran into the Philadelphia night

Left the lady and the president at the dining table.

Didn't you know the lady would cry?

Didn't you know the president would think you ungrateful?

You were his money walking out the door

Why you run Ona Judge?

Didn't you know being a slave in the President's House was grand?

Didn't you know you broke the law?

Didn't you know George Washington would send men after you?

You knew you were more . . .

Than a ten-dollar pet

The lady wanted back

In an attic, basement, or room no one could see

You waited for the boat

To carry you on the Underground sea

Where your future would not be enslaved

For the rest of your days

They called you a runaway, a fugitive

But Liberty rang for you

You dreamed a dream

You would make true

To read, to write

To do what you want, to go where you like

To make sure your children would not be enslaved

Like you

Like your mother

Your grandmother, and her mother, too?

Is that why you ran?

Then run, Ona Judge, *run*

AUTHOR'S NOTE

Ona or Oney Judge* was about twenty-three when she emancipated herself from the President's House in Philadelphia. From the age of ten she worked in the Washington households in Mount Vernon, New York City, and Philadelphia. She was first a playmate for the Washingtons' grandchildren, then later a seamstress or "mistress of her needle" and a personal servant to Martha Washington. Ona was blessed with intelligence, deportment, and effort, but was enslaved by the family that had brought independence and freedom to America. When told that she would

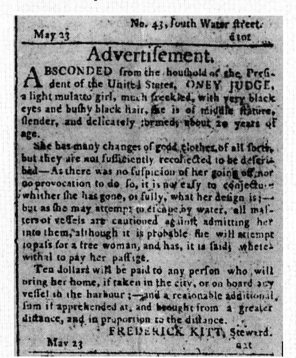

be a wedding gift to one of Martha's granddaughters, Ona decided to risk her life and flee. Many African Americans were never able to escape slavery. But with the help of abolitionists, both Black and white, Ona fled to New Hampshire, the state that proclaimed "Live Free or Die." Ona Judge chose the hard life of a fugitive runaway rather than remain an enslaved servant to the Washington family.

---

* I have used the name Ona in telling of her daring escape. However, Washington's reward advertisement called her by her childhood diminutive, Oney, even though she was an adult when she fled enslavement. The National Park Service at Mount Vernon and the City of Philadelphia's President's House site also referred to her as Oney because the Washingtons did.

TIMELINE

1759   The widow Martha Custis, the wealthiest woman in Virginia, marries George Washington and moves to his Mount Vernon plantation. She brings eighty enslaved African Americans, including her seamstress, Betty, and Betty's two-year-old son, Austin.

1773   Ona Judge is born to Betty. Her father is a white indentured servant.

1776   The Declaration of Independence signed in Philadelphia declares, "All men are created equal." The Declaration does not include white women, African Americans, or Native Americans.

1788   The U.S. Constitution is ratified. In reference to slavery, the authors use the term "Person held to Service or Labour."

1789   George Washington is elected president and moves to New York City, the seat of the federal government at the time. Martha Washington takes sixteen-year-old Ona Judge with her as well as Ona's thirty-two-year-old brother, Austin. Betty is not asked if her daughter can be taken from Mount Vernon, and Austin is forced to leave his wife and children behind.

1790   The federal government relocates to Philadelphia. Ona and Austin are moved to Philadelphia and are two of the ten enslaved Americans living in the President's House.

1793   President Washington signs the first federal Fugitive Slave Act. The law allows a slave master to seize runaways in free states.

1796   Ona Judge learns she is going to be given as a wedding gift to Martha Washington's granddaughter Eliza. With the help of unknown free African Americans, Ona hides in Philadelphia while waiting for a white sea captain to ferry her to New Hampshire.

BIBLIOGRAPHY

Chernow, Ron. *Washington: A Life*. New York: Penguin, 2010.

Dunbar, Erica Armstrong. *Never Caught: The Washingtons' Relentless Pursuit of Their Runaway Slave, Ona Judge*. New York: Simon & Schuster, 2017.

Gerson, Evelyn B. "A Thirst for Complete Freedom: Why Fugitive Slave Ona Judge Staines Never Returned to Her Master, President George Washington." Master's Thesis, Harvard University, 2000.

McClafferty, Carla Killough. *Buried Lives: Enslaved People of George Washington's Mount Vernon*. New York: Penguin, 2018.

The Pennsylvania Gazette, Philadelphia, Pennsylvania, May 24, 1796.

Sammons, Mark J., and Valerie Cunningham. *Black Portsmouth: Three Centuries of African-American Heritage*. Durham, University of New Hampshire Press, 2004.

Schoelwer, Susan P. (Ed.) *Lives Bound Together: Slavery at George Washington's Mount Vernon*. Mount Vernon Ladies Association, 2018.

Schwartz, Marie Jenkins. *Ties That Bound: Founding First Ladies and Slaves*. Chicago: University of Chicago Press, 2017.

Sherburne, Michelle Arnosky. *Slavery & the Underground Railroad in New Hampshire*. Charleston, SC: History Press, 2016.

Wiencek, Henry. *An Imperfect God: George Washington, His Slaves, and the Creation of America*. New York: Farrar, Straus & Giroux, 2003.

AUTHOR'S ACKNOWLEDGMENTS

I am grateful to the Highlights Foundation Workshop, where I was encouraged by Kathryn Erskine, Padma Venkatraman, and Alma Fullerton to develop this story. Thanks to the talent of Keith Mallett and the careful guidance of Grace Kendall and Caryn Wiseman, this book moved from an idea in my head to the one in your hands. And special thanks to Roz McPherson for the guided tour of the President's House site, and to David Weir for the private tour of Mount Vernon, pointing out where it is likely Ona and her mother, Betty, lived.

ARTIST'S ACKNOWLEDGMENTS

Thanks to Ray for introducing me to Ona Judge. Special thanks to Grace and Aram for their guidance in helping me to share her remarkable story.

A NOTE ON STYLE

I used rhetorical questions as a poetic structure through which to tell Ona's story of escape. During slavery—and even now—people questioned why an enslaved person in such a fine home would want to leave. But slavery is slavery, whether it takes place in a field or the President's House. In my poem, I reclaim those questions to show the inherent humanity of the enslaved.

PLACES TO VISIT

African American Museum in Philadelphia, Pennsylvania

aampmuseum.org

National Museum of African American History and Culture, Washington, DC

nmaahc.si.edu

Museum of the American Revolution, Philadelphia, Pennsylvania

amrevmuseum.org

Black Heritage Trail of New Hampshire, Portsmouth, New Hampshire

blackheritagetrailnh.org

The President's House, Philadelphia, Pennsylvania

ushistory.org/presidentshouse/index.php